ISBN 978-0-484-62004-8
PIBN 10192568

This book is a reproduction of an important historical work. Forgotten Books uses state-of-the-art technology to digitally reconstruct the work, preserving the original format whilst repairing imperfections present in the aged copy. In rare cases, an imperfection in the original, such as a blemish or missing page, may be replicated in our edition. We do, however, repair the vast majority of imperfections successfully; any imperfections that remain are intentionally left to preserve the state of such historical works.

SONGS
FROM THE WAYSIDE

BY

NINETTE M. LOWATER

A Book of Verse

The royal sun, the beauty of the night,
  The waters, moaning with mysterious fear,
The flitting wind, with touches soft and light,
The swaying trees, the blossoms fair and bright—
  All have a message for the listening ear.

Copyright 1906, by the Author

THE SUN PRESS,
SPRING VALLEY, WIS.

ACKNOWLEDGEMENT

Nearly all the poems in this volume have appeared previously in *Leslie's Monthly, The Youth's Companion, The New York Sun, The. New York Herald, Smart Set, The Churchman, Midland Monthly,* and other magazines and periodicals. Their kind permission to reprint is hereby acknowledged.

This book is Dedicated

to

The Friends

whose Love and Sympathy

have inspired it

MRS. NINETTE M. LOWATER

OCCASIONAL POEMS

Memory

O Memory, bind fast with many a coil
  The wealth of years which I have given to you;
  If to my faith and trust you prove untrue,
What have I left, of all a lifetime's spoil?

I gave you pictures of the far-off sea,
  Lashed by wild winds, or still as if asleep;
  Of rivers poising for a downward leap,
Or winding through still valleys, calm and free.

I gave you pictures of great fields of grain,
  Rippling like waves beneath the western
    breeze;
  Of forests yet unspoiled, whose giant trees
Have braved unharmed a century's wind and rain.

And more than these, I gave into your hold
  Tones that were sweet and faces that were
    dear,
  The touch of hands that dried each childish
    tear,
Now hidden deep beneath the churchyard's mould.

Dear words from tongues that speak, alas! no more,
  Dear looks from eyes long closed upon earth's
    strife;
  Keep them, I pray, and guard them all my life;
O Memory, hold fast my golden store.

The Song of Labor

I sing the song of the workman;
    The joy of the man whose hand
Leaps to fulfil, with practised skill,
    The keen, sure brain's demand;
Who knows the joy of creation,
    Who stands with the Lord as one,
Sees what was wrought from hidden thought,
    And can say of his work, "Well done!"

Others may seek for rank and wealth,
    And search the wide world through;
He knows the deep where grand thoughts sleep,
    Which Tubal Cain once knew.
Beauty may lie in a woman's eye,
    And dwell on her lips so sweet—
It lives as well in the engine's swell,
    And the piston's throbbing beat.

The arch which defies the river's flood
    And holds its waves in check,
Is fair as the line where tresses twine,
    Or the curve of a snowy neck.
And he who can feel such beauty's power,
    And bid it live and move,
Knows a deeper bliss than a maiden's kiss
    Can give to the heart of love.

Some must lie soft and feed daintily,
    Or the soul of them makes moan;
But little he heeds who finds his needs
    In the maker's joy alone.

Sorrow and pain may come to him—
    They surely come to all—
But ever he feels a strength that steels
    His heart to the shafts that fall.

He gladly greets the coming years;
    They bring him added skill.
He feels no ruth for the loss of youth;
    His goal is nearer still.
And only this he asks of fate—
    That he may keep his dower
Of strength and will, and labor's skill
    Unto his life's last hour.

The Place of My Desire

Through many weary years,
    From dawn to sunset's fire,
I've sought, with pain and tears,
    The Place of my Desire.

Perhaps they told me wrong,
    Perhaps I missed the road;
Still with a purpose strong
    I seek that fair abode.

I see it in my dreams—
    How pleasant, and how fair!
Its towers, with golden gleams,
    Shine through the cloudless air.

There is no hated task,
    There only friendships stay;

There are the joys I ask,
   The year is always May.
O, Place of my Desire!
   Since but in dreams I take
The path that leads me nigher,
   O, may I never wake!

The World's Great Peace

I saw the navies of the allied world
   Riding at ease within a sheltered bay;
   In peace and quiet, side by side they lay,
For all the battle-flags at last were furled.
The angry cannon stood, all still and grim,
   Like dogs in leash straining to find a foe;
   Yet all the ports were closed, and to and fro
The ships swayed lightly on the ocean's rim.
Never again their thunder shall declare
   Ruin and death for helpless shore and land;
   They kept the peace of seas from strand to
      strand,
And bandit cruisers feared to leave their lair.
Allied in peace, each nation claimed their aid
   Only against the enemies of all;
   No guardian fortress from their fire shall fall,
And only crime hides from them, sore afraid.

Alas! The dawning, with its golden gleam,
   Awoke me to a world where wars increase;
   The keepers of the allied world's great peace
Passed with my dream—ah, was it but a dream?

Contentment

My garden is a tiny plot,
    Where winds have barely room to play,
A quiet, hidden little spot,
    Wherein alone for hours I stay.

Few flowers are there—you who may pass
    Where blossoms dream their life away
In rank on rank beneath the glass,
    Would find them scarce one glance repay.

But for me each one hides the gold
    Of summer in its chalice fair;
And when my one red rose I hold,
    My June is crowned with rapture rare.

Song of a Bird

Just a little bit of feather
And life and song, all held together
By a heart almost too small to beat,
With cobweb wings and twinkling feet.
Where, in a body as small as this,
Does he store the passion of joy and bliss,
Of life in its utmost ecstasy,
Which his little throat pours out to me?
No shadow of fear his heart can know,
Or that perfect music could not flow
So sweet, so clear, so exultingly,
As light as the winds, as wild and free!
He is surely the heart of the summer weather,
Life, joy, and song, in a bit of feather!

The Corn

A song of the corn, the sturdy corn, which bright-
  ens this land of ours:
Its tender green in the early spring is fairer than
  blossoming flowers;
It amber silk,, with its glossy sheen, is fit for a
  fairy's loom,
And dearer its dimpled, golden ears than the rose
  or lily's bloom,
For they bear the promise of happy hours to the
  man who toils for bread,
When he need not fear that his little ones must go
  to sleep unfed.

There are lovely flowers in this land of ours, wher-
  ever the foot may fall,
The tongue and the ear alike would tire, should I
  try to tell them all,
From the arbutus on Atlantic shores to the golden
  poppy's gleams,
As bright as the metal which lies at its roots by
  Californian streams;
But never a flower such gifts has gained from the
  sun and dews of morn,
Or stands more fair in the summer air than the
  blessed, golden corn!

Angels of the Household

Not they who cluster round the hearth
    With cheerful looks and smiles,
Who charm away our care and grief
    With loving words and wiles;
Upon whose cheek the bloom of health
    Has left the roseate glow—
No, these are not the angels sent
    To guide our steps below.

For often we forget that life
    Is but a passing day,
That all its bliss, its joys and hopes,
    Like mist will fade away,
And strive to win for those we love
    Pride's highest rank and name,
Forgetting that the silent grave
    Knows not of earthly fame.

But when the twilight shadows fall
    Upon the weary earth,
When e'en the children leave their play,
    And hush their noisy mirth,
Then memory o'er our heartstrings sweeps
    Her shadowy, mystic wand,
And those we loved in other days
    Again beside us stand.

Again our mother's loving voice
    With music cheers our way;
Once more we clasp the prattling babe
    We lost but yesterday;

And every love that heaven has caught
    From earth's unkindly shore,
Again to us in fancy comes,
    To bless us, as of yore.

And when by earthly cares recalled
    We put our dreams away,
How worthless seems the dross of earth
    Which over us held sway.
Our hearts are purer than they were,
    And free from passion's tides;
The dearly loved, but early lost—
    They are our angel guides.

Nature's Miracle

He who loves not a noble tree
No fellowship may claim from me.

Deep in the earth its great roots spread,
But heaven's own blue surrounds its head.

It holds the joys of summer's morn,
The strength of winter's wildness born.

God's birds find shelter in its arms,
Secure from everything that harms.

It bows when south winds wander past,
But breasts unharmed the fiercest blast.

'Tis Nature's miracle to me,
Her fairest work—a noble tree.

The Blizzard

In the Polar night, with its snows eternal,
    Of its cold and darkness I was born;
To me came the knowledge of meadows vernal,
    And I left my lair accursed and forlorn.

Swift were the wings that southward bore me,
    Far and wide spread my desolate track;
I found not the South, for it fled before me,
    And death and destruction were close at my
        back.

Oh, how I laughed, when the grass in the valley
    Blackened and withered beneath my tread!
I laughed when I heard the south wind rally
    His forces to hurl at my conquering head.

But my strong wings drooped, and fear assailed me,
    My soul grew sick with the scent of flowers;
I fled to the North, which never failed me,
    Away from the weakening southland bowers.

Here I crouch in my desolate eyrie,
    Till strength shall come to my wings again,
Till the day when, no longer faint and weary,
    I shall visit again the homes of men!

A Song of Nature

Two things are ever dear to me—
A river and a noble tree.

Two things are always sweet to know—
The sun, and south winds when they blow.

Two things the world with beauty fill—
The red rose and the whip-poor-will.

Two things are earth's supreme delight—
A rainbow and the stars at night.

An Invocation

O, spirit of the summer time,
　　Bring back the verdue to the hills,
And from the winter's frost and rime
　　Free the unhappy, captive rills.

Unbind the lances of the storm,
　　Set free the sweet, imprisoned rain.
Where now the snow's battalions form
　　Let bud and bloom appear again.

Circumstance

Say what we may, do what we will,
Circumstance is our master still;
    Lord of us all, it sets the bounds
    Through which we toil in weary rounds.
Who thinks to force its firm-set bars
As well might overleap the stars;
    Who wins, however keen his wit,
    May know he is its favorite.

Love

Love is the touchstone of the noble soul;
    If e'er it harbored one dishonoring thought,
    Or deed unworthy to completion wrought,
It shrinks abashed from clear-eyed Love's control.

The idols which it worshipped seem but clay,
    The treasures which it cherished fairy gold,
    Which vanishes from e'en the closest hold;
And like dim stars which pale before the day

Are all affections which it once held dear.
    It counts no time but hours the loved one shares;
    No theme but one dear name pervades its prayers;
It fears no darkness so that love shines clear.

All which it once desired is now forgot;
    Ambition, pride, unto their master bow.
    And heaven and hell have but one meaning
        now—
The place where Love is, or where he is not!

The Call

"Come," said a voice to the poet, as he sought an
    elusive rhyme
One night when the world was sleeping, in the
    heart of the sweet May-time;
"Oh, how can I come?" he answered, "let me
    alone, I pray,
For the verse I now am weaving the hearts of men
    will sway."
"Come," said the voice to the statesman, as he
    stood in the Senate hall,
And men moved on at his bidding, as troops at a
    bugle call;
"How can I come?" he answered, "my sun at its
    zenith stands—
Ere it sets my name shall be spoken through all
    the earth's wide lands."
"Come," said the voice to a mother with her chil-
    dren at her knee,
Dreaming how safe and happy their life at her side
    should be;
"Oh, I cannot come," she answered; "I pray you,
    let me stay—
For how can I leave my darlings to wander far
    away?"
No other word was spoken, but the poet dropped
    his pen,
The statesman's name was heard no more upon
    the lips of men,
The children found no mother, though they called

with sobbing breath—
For the voice which spoke all must obey—it was
the voice of Death.

Life

They lived, they loved, they wrought
In fair domains of thought,
Or grim want's battlefield,
Where manhood is revealed;
Then passed; and few can say
Where once they stood, to-day;
And this is the epitome
Of all that has been, or shall be.

My Lady Spring

My Lady Spring came walking in,
    Only the other day;
So long we looked, so late she staid,
    We feared she'd missed the way.

"O Lady Spring, dear Lady Spring,
    Why did you make us wait?
If you had come a month ago
    You still had been too late."

But Lady Spring said not a word—
    She only turned and smiled;
Ah!   Well she knew no one could chide,
    By such a look beguiled.

The Winds

The winds are up, the winds are out,
    What is the use for men to strive?
See how they beat the waves about,
    And toss the ships as though alive.

Here stood a city in their path,
    Where oft they stopped to rest and play;
Last night they came in stress and wrath,
    And not a soul was left to pray.

Who guides their courses fleet and free?
    Who knows the ways by which they come?
And when they charge o'er land and sea,
    Who turns them backward to their home?

The Tempest

The war-ships of the tempest
    Are sweeping through the sky;
We listen to their booming guns,
    And see their pennons fly.

They are the sky's Armada,
    Which nothing can withstand;
The only orders they obey
    Are given by God's own hand.

And when His hand is lifted
    To bid their fury cease,
The Bow of Promise lights the clouds—
    The signal of His peace.

An Easter Song

I lay awake at midnight before the Easter day,
I saw the stars shine brightly along the milky way.
The scent of tender blossms filled all the dewy air,
The world with reverent gladness was quiet, as in
     prayer.
Earth's organ tones were silent, but through the
     pine's dark crest
There ran an eager whisper of happiest unrest.
I thought of that dark evening long centuries ago,
When night closed down with horror upon the
     world's great woe.
The black night saw the Saviour lie sleeping in
     the grave,
And hearts grew faint with terror, for there was
     none to save.
But joy came with the morning, light chased away
     the gloom—
He was not dead, or sleeping, but risen from the
     tomb.
Would I had heard the singing of birds upon that
     day,
Had seen the happy blossoms, or known what
     south winds say.
But while I waked and wondered the Easter
     morning broke,
And all earth's myriad voices in sweetest music
     woke.
"The Lord, the Lord has risen," the happy birds
     proclaim,

"Fill all the world with singing, in glory to His
name."
O, heart of mine, awake from silence and from
sleep,
Join in the swelling chorus—your soul's glad
Easter keep.
Bind offerings of lilies upon His temple stairs,
And He who loves the blossoms will hearken to
your prayers.
And when unto your duties you tread the accus-
tomed way,
Keep in your heart His promise—be each an
Easter day.

Twilight

A golden glory in the sky,
  Mirrored in waves which strive no more;
The cry of night-birds, flitting by,
  And lo! the day is o'er.

The crescent moon-disc, rising slow,
  With one attendant, radiant sphere;
A cloud across the sunset's glow,
  And lo! the night is here.

King Wheat

You may tell of your armored cruisers,
    And your great ships of the line;
And swift or slow may steamers go
    Across the billowy brine.
Like thunder may the cannons boom
    To greet their flags unfurled,
And hour for hour, they may have power
    To rule the frightened world.

From ocean shore to ocean shore
    Lie lines of gleaming steel,
And night or day, we hear alway
    The ring of rushing wheel;
Though buffalo have left the plain,
    And Indian tents are furled,
Nor steam nor hand at wealth's command
    Can rule the busy world.

But where the hillside rises fair
    In terraces of green,
And on the plain, where wind and rain
    Sweep fields of golden sheen,
Where sturdy yellow stalks arise,
    With bannered heads unfurled,
Here you may greet the great King Wheat,
    The ruler of the world.

Oh, hills may shake and vales resound
    Beneath the flying car,
And driven by steam and winds a-beam
    Our ships ride fast and far;

Cities may crumble 'neath the guns
   Which guard our flag unfurled,
Yet all shall greet—at last—King Wheat,
   For hunger rules the world.

My Song

Once in my early youth I knew a song,
   I know not how I learned it now, or when;
But oh, it was so sweet! If I had sung
   The world perforce must all have listened then.
But many a pathway lured my willing feet,
   And oft I tarried long at pleasure's gate;
And when I heard a whisper, "You should sing,"
   I said "It will be sweeter if I wait."

But when the length'ning shadows eastward turned,
   And heavier grew the burden I must bear,
I said "I shall forget it if I wait,
   Now I must sing my song, so sweet and rare."
But ah, I had forgotten! And the world,
   Restless and eager, would not turn aside;
None heard the faint, uncertain notes which rose,
   Trembled and faltered, and in silence died.

The Passing of Summer

All garlanded with golden grain,
    And bearing fruits and berries red,
The Summer followed those great streams
    By which the gulf is fed.

With her the singing birds have gone,
    And all the dainty woodland flowers;
There is a shadow on the noon,
    A hush upon the bowers.

No more the yellow sun rides high
    And calls on sluggards to arise;
We watch and wait to see him drive
    The pale moon from the skies.

The trees are gay with painted leaves,
    The crickets fiddle loud and shrill,
But the far path that summer took
    Is lone and lonely still.

Earth, the Beautiful

I think the time will never be
When earth will not seem fair to me.
If I may see the arching sky,
With fleecy cloud-wrack floating by;
A tree with green, uplifted head,
And clover in its shadow spread;
Or see a river's stately flight,
Its ripples dancing in the light;
Though keen my sorrow, deep my woe,

Yet happiness my heart must know.
Or if to sleepless eyes no ray
Should enter from the brighest day
If I might smell a violet
My darkened way I should forget,
And in my fancy see once more
The woodland aisles with boughs arched o'er,
And gathered thickly round my feet
The bending wild flowers, fair and sweet.
Or if my hand might hold a rose,
The garden gate would swift unclose,
And rank on rank would bloom for me
Far fairer flowers than now I see.
The ocean waves would sing for me
Their mournful, vibrant symphony;
And when in organ tones arise
Storm voices grandly to the skies,
My puny woe, ashamed to stay,
With them would quickly pass away,
And in the deep succeeding calm,
My soul would join in nature's psalm.

After

The merry Christmas tide is past,
　　The chiming New Year bells are still;
And veiled by memory's circling mist,
　　The old year passes down the hill.

On to life's lotus-land he goes—
　. The time of youth, when all was fair;
Already seem his sorrows less,
　　His pleasures great beyond compare.

And often in the future days,
　　Remembrance of his sunny hours
Will make us sigh for gladness past,
　　As Autumn sighs for springtime flowers.

But now we turn from him away
　　And gaze adown the path that lies
Before us, bright with fancy gleams
　　Beneath hope's fair unclouded skies.

But ever through the songs of mirth
　　This minor, sad refrain we hear;
"Sometime a glad New Year will dawn,
　　And I, alas! shall not be here!"

The Storm

The storm is abroad in its wrath and might—
　　God pity the souls at sea;
Oh, ye who kneel down in your homes to-night,
　　Give thanks for your safe roof-tree.

My Little Maid with Laughing Eyes

There's a new grave on the hill tonight
Where yester-morn the grass grew bright,
And snow-white waving daisies hid
The cricket and the katy-did;
Now deep within its shadows lies
My little maid with laughing eyes;
She sleeps beneath the mound so bare,
And oh, my heart lies buried there.
      Oh, little maid with laughing eyes,
        And sunshine in your silken hair,
      You sweetly sleep, while long hours creep,
        But oh, my heart lies buried there.

Her little feet will never tread
The thorny paths where mine have bled;
No shade of sorrow or of sin
Will hide those laughing eyes within;
No frost of years shall touch one tress,
Or dim its glorious loveliness;
Her sleep is sweet, with visions fair,
But oh, my heart lies buried there.
      Oh, little maid with laughing eyes,
        And sunshine in your silken hair,
      So sweet your sleep I may not weep,
        But oh, my heart lies buried there.

The Aurora Borealis

The rose of winter blossoms in the sky;
High o'er the cloudless arch its petals lie;
Such changing hues no earth-flower ever wore,
But in an hour it fades—to bloom no more.

Poetry

No word of all the languages can tell what it may
     be;
They cannot make us understand its spirit fine and
     free.
We only know it by the flame it kindles in the
     heart,
Which consecrates us evermore its high priest,
     set apart.
Elusive as the wandering wind, or as the wild
     flower's breath,
Yet all things earthly it defies—it triumphs over
     death!

After the Snow

A strange new world spreads out before my eyes,
    A world of silence and of mystery;
Where'er I turn I meet some new surprise,
    Some evanescent beauty waiting me;
What weird enchanter waved his magic wand,
And changed to marble all the living land?

The Death Song of the Trees

"We are doomed," sighed the trees, "for ever and
    ever come nigher
The axe and the biting saw, and the all-devouring
    fire.
We are strong to meet our fate, but woe for the
    innocent things
Which have lived their happy lives in the peace
    our shelter brings.
The deer will find no refuge from the hunter's
    deadly gun,
The frail wild flowers will wither in the glare of the
    noonday sun;
The streams will dry at their fountains, the nest-
    ling birds must go,
The whole fair land will be stricken with loneliness
    and woe.
No more to the parching southland will the winds
    bring cooling balm;
They will pass an arid desert, with death in its
    changeless calm.

"Alas," sighed the trees together—the wail swept
    on and on—
"Alas for the beautiful land, when its guardian
    trees are gone!"

One Day

Oh, day of days!   If I had known
Before thy wondrous light had flown,
Or if I had but dimly guessed
With thee would pass all peace and rest,
Then had I set each hour of thine
In memory's most sacred shrine.

Swiftly the minutes sped away,
And brought the close of that fair day;
With tender words and clasping hands
We parted on the golden sands,
And love, alas, henceforth can be
Only a memory to me.

Through all that day, whose flying hours
Seemed shining links in chains of flowers,
Beside·us walked the spectre, Death,
With pallid cheek and icy breath,
And yet no step, no shadow grim,
One moment turned our thoughts to him.

Oh, day of days!   Forevermore
I live in thought thy minutes o'er,
Striving to win some tone or look
From dim Oblivion's closing book,
And sighing, "Oh, that I had known
Before thy shining hours had flown!"

Spring Poetry

They say that poets never
    Should sing of budding spring;
I wonder if they ever
    Have heard the robins sing,
Or found the wind-flowers growing
    Upon a hillside gray,
Where snows were lately blowing,
    And spring seemed far away.

Let those talk on who never
    Have seen the catkins start,
Fed from the tide that ever
    Flows through the tree's green heart;
Who never saw earth brighten
    When south winds come to stay,
Or felt their own heart lighten
    When blue skies follow gray.

But we who know the glory
    When earth awakes from sleep,
Who hear the new-old story
    Told in the river's leap,
When first, its ice-bonds riven,
    It moves, a sentient thing—
We to whom this is given
    May surely sing of spring.

The City of No Night

The day passed through the twilight's open bars,
    And in the darkened sky the pale moon shone,
    The stately Night claimed her imperial throne;
And from her shadow gleamed the waiting stars.
Yet knew the city nothing of the Night.—
    A clear, white splendor burned above the way,
    Nearer and softer than the orb of day,
And darkness fled before its radiant light.

Hidden and chained, the dynamos complain,
    And murmur, yet the master's will obey;
    Theirs is the task to steal the light of day,
And set men free from night's insiduous reign;
    With this his servant, fettered to his will,
    Man conquers darkness, and the day stands still.

The Old Oak Tree

The sweetest thing of earth to me
Is the south wind in the old oak tree.

It moves the branches to and fro;
The shadows dance on the grass below.

The leaves move lightly in the air—
Their rustle seems a whispered prayer.

Deep in the tangled grass I lie,
Seeing but glimpses of the sky.

So thick the green leaves are above,
So light, so soft, the breezes move,

I wonder not that men have stood
Before some giant of the wood,

And made it of their prayers a shrine,
Deeming it held a soul divine.

Morning

Over the clear, deep blue of the sky a film of silver
    steals,
And lower in the star-gemmed west the radiant
    moon-disc wheels.

No earth can I see around me, only an opal mist,
Which in the horizon's verge afar changes to
    amethyst.

One by one the stars grow pale, and a blush like
    the heart of a rose
Springs from the mist to the eastern sky, and
    clings, and deepens, and grows.

Behold, a shaft of golden light, which pierces the
    fog-wrack white.
The trees lift up their stately heads, and earth is
    bathed in light.

I have seen the world created—it is pure, and fair
    and new;
God said again "Let there be light," and lo, the
    sun burst through.

The Dasher Churn

Down by the spring in the shade of the trees,
　I churn my cream in the cool of the day;
Many and many a time I've seen
　My grandmother churn in the selfsame way.

Since then, full many a patent churn
　Has lived its life and had its day;
But in spite of all that has come and gone,
　I churn my cream in the old-time way.

The butter comes in a golden ball,
　Fresh and sweet as the flowers in May;
Was it better in the days gone by?
　Is it better in the newer way?

And so there is many an old time thing
　Which you think is buried and gone for aye:
But you will find that it's living yet,
　Like the dasher churn I use to-day.

Truth and honor and noble lives—
　They are out of fashion now, you say—
But the germ in every heart survives
　And the world grows better day by day.

The Water

What is it that aileth the waters—the river, the
    lake, the sea?
Forever a miserere they chant of a grief to be.
They have garnered the fear and terror from aeons
    of pain and woe,
And from land to land go sobbing in minors weird
    and low.
Only the heart sore-stricken by sorrow's heavy
    · hand
Can hear below the rythm, interpret, and under-
    stand;
Only the soul grown hopeless can hear again and
    again
To earth's cry of baffled longing, the water's sad ·
    "Amen."

Too Late

Too late!   The words came sounding through the
    ages,
  Filled with the burdens of all human life;
Too late to turn Love's open, roseate pages,
  Too late to quench the flames of cruel strife.
Too late for friendships slipped away forever,
  For gracious deeds, by loving kindness sped;
Ah, happiest of all are they who never
  Have cried "too late" above the unheeding dead.

Swift moves the hand of Time across the dial!
  This hour is thine—thy certain gift from fate;
It has no space for respite or re-trial—
  Be thine the boon to find it not too late.

Lilies

Lilies, lilies red and gold, lilies white as snow,
Which is fairest of them all—who can ever know?
Yet, methinks this creamy one with the waxen cup
Saw our Savior's loving glance when he took it up,
And has kept it in its heart through the Summer's
    glow,
And has thought of that alone, underneath the snow!

The Reapers

I will sing you a song of a reaper; his tireless
    scythe he swings,
With the clover blooms around him lying in broken
    rings;
The air grows faint and heavy with the weight of
    their perfumed breath,
And their rosy hues fade out beneath the unspar-
    ing hand of death.

I will sing you a song of a reaper; he moves o'er
    the uplands brown,
And wherever his sickle flashes the ranks of the
    corn fall down;
Yesterday tall and stately it stood in its ripened
    pride—
To-day it is lying helpless and bound on the bare
    hillside.

I will sing you a song of a reaper; through the
    forest his ax-stroke rings,
Where stand the oaks which braved the storms
    through the reigns of a hundred kings;
Deep have the great roots clasped the earth, the
    grand heads seek the sky,
But puny man has doomed them, and beneath his
    hand they die.

I will sing you a song of a reaper; his sickle hath
    no man seen,
We hear not his step on the upland, or down on
    the meadows green;

But he ever moves among us, through the city and
       forest deep,
And they whom his finger touches in silence his
       secret keep.

But the corn which bowed down to the reaper, and
       the fragrant grass laid low,
Fed the hungry kine and their master when the
       north winds brought the snow.
And the trees which the wind and lightning had
       spared these many years
Have made a dwelling-place for man, where he
       rests, secure from fears.

And the Master hath sent forth the reaper who
       gathers the fair and dear,
He will add them to His treasure, which He keeps
       to His hand anear;
And no more than the corn or the clover, or the
       stately forest tree,
Can we tell where He will use them—but the
       Master holds the key.

The Crowded Hour

I do not love the city's roar,
    Like hungry beasts unsatisfied;
Its canoned streets where evermore
    Pours back and forth a human tide;

I do not love the way that lies
    Along the shadowed, sunless street;
The stabbing stare of stranger eyes,
    The ceaseless din of stranger feet;

I stifle in the lifeless air,
    The arch above is strange to me;
I long to see the meadows fair,
    Where heaven's own winds may wander free;

I long to see the fleckless skies
    Bend o'er me, like a jeweled cup,
To see the unveiled sun arise,
    And to the stars at night look up.

Give me the sweet companionship
    Of bird, and bee, and wayside flower;
Let me from Nature's chalice sip,
    And with her live my crowded hour!

Thanksgiving

Thank God for Love.   Though one kind heart alone
Respond with true affection to your own;
Though all beside unheeding pass you by,
Yet light divine illumes your earthly sky—
   Thank God for Love!

Thank God for Life.   Though rough the path you
  know,
Though well acquaint with poverty and woe,
While you at morn the earth's fair face behold,
While night still spreads her pomp of rose and
  gold—
   Thank God for Life!

Thank God for Death.   After the summer hours
Beneath the snow sleep all the weary flowers;
So, after all Life's pains and joys are past,
Shall Death bring kindly rest for all at last—
   Thank God for Death!

In An Ancient Wood

I stood within a winding woodland aisle,
With trees like pillars wrought with wondrous wile;
Vines wreathed them, draped with curious droop
       and turn,
And deep their bases sank amid the fern.
From pale flower-censers, slowly swinging there,
A fragrance filled the cool, illumined air;
Wandering through arches deep, mysterious, dim,
Tones echoed sweet as song of seraphim;
Low, penetrating, harmonies unordered, new,
With choruses triumphant breaking through;
They filled my heart, as waters fill the sea,
And from life's galling bonds my soul rose free.

In this undesecrated grove, alone,
I found a temple unto man unknown,
With roof and buttress, column, architrave,
Nobler than human skill e'er planned or gave,
Filled with illusive fragrance of the leaf
And wood-flower, whose frail life is sweet as brief;
I heard the birds, to whom alone is given
To sing on earth the harmonies of heaven;
Thus near to nature, like our earlier race,
I lost the greed of gold and love of place;
A higher level my glad spirit found—
Then knew I that I stood on holy ground.

A Song of Hope

Beyond the narrow limit which marks our mortal
marge
Dwell they once prisoned with us, whom death has
set at large.
Not in some walled-in city beyond our planet's ken
Bide they who once were with us, but in the homes
of men.
Unseen they move among us; we pass them on
the stair;
At eve they sit among us, in each accustomed
chair;
But to the words they utter our ears are deaf and
sealed;
Not unto eyes earth-shadowed is one dear face
revealed.
But in each soul's recesses they touch a chord
which thrills,
E'en as the rain-drop reaches the pulses of the hills.

The Night Cometh

Sometime a day shall dawn for thee
In which thine eyes no change may see;
The sun will shine, with wonted grace,
On every dear, familiar place;
No cloud will veil its skies with gloom,
Yet it shall be thy day of doom.

Thy life web shall unfinished stand
Where falls the shuttle from thy hand;
No loving deed can add its gold,
No kindly word, in silver told,
May broider its design for thee—
Once stopped, the loom shall idle be.

Then, since each morn may bring the day
When unseen hands thy work shall stay,
Let every act and word of thine
Fulfil the harmonious design;
Weave life's strange web with watchful care—
Each thread may be the last one there.

The Court of War

Not all an evil is war, grim and stern,
It is the sword, swift, keen, which pierces through
The shell of wrong, the ancient or the new,
And brings to judgment lands that will not learn.
It is the mighty, unchained force, which draws
All hidden tyrany to fullest light,
The Court of Last Appeal to God and right,
Where each stakes life and freedom for his cause.

And he who offers this, when duty calls
To save his country's honor, serve her need,
Who meets death unafraid—whate'er befalls,
Has he not gained the heighth of human deed?
He has known all that life can hold to give,
And if he die, has felt what 'tis to live.

My Valentine

The sun comes shining up the sky;
   Its warmth gives promise of the spring:
Though cold and white the snowdrifts lie,
   The happy birds begin to sing.
But in my heart no sweet chimes ring,
I feel no token of Love's spring;
   Shine out, O maiden, maiden mine,
   Upon your lonely Valentine.

Through all the day, like silver bells,
   The old rhyme in my heart has rung;
Like water in unfailing wells,
   The love in it is ever young;
"The rose is red, the violet blue,
The pink is sweet, and so are you."
   O listen, maiden, maiden mine,
   So sings your loving Valentine.

Dispel the night that round me lies!
   Shine out, O sun that makes my spring!
Look kindly with those lovely eyes,
   Whence Cupid's arrows gain their sting!
She comes—how balmy sweet the air!
She smiles—the earth is passing fair!
   With loving glance and hand in mine,
   I've won her for my Valentine.

SONNETS

The Tide of Years

Come back, O Youth, with all your hopes and
    fears ˙
    Across the years which thickly intervene;
    I do not ask your hair of silken sheen,
Your rosy cheeks, or eyes that shine through tears;
Nay—though this mirrored visage strange appears,
    Like some pale mask which rudely comes between
    And hides the face so long and often seen,
For this I do not call across the years.

But give me back the joy and courage high,
    The bounding pulse, the ardent soul of yore,
    The hope I knew when long life spread before,
And all Life's gifts seemed in my path to lie.
Let Age pile frost on my devoted head,
    So thou, O Youth, reign in my heart instead.

A Vision of Life

I saw a mighty caravan with slow
    Steps move across a bare and wind-swept plain;
    As wave crowds wave upon the tossing main,
So each his brother drove with threat and blow.
Far in the west the mist hung thick and low,
    Yet on they moved, and none turned back again,
    Eastward, from purple shades swept on the
        train— ˙
Whether or whence no watching eye might know.

Long gazed I on the soft and shrouding mist

Which wavered, thinned, and almost drew aside,
With hues that changed from gray to amethyst;
    And portals which held fast the living tide,
Nor knew, until I felt its folds touch me,
    That I was one of that strange company.

A Summer Day

To lie in clover and watch the sky
    As the sun nears the gateway of the west,
    While like tall galleons seeking home and rest,
The bright clouds gather and roll swiftly by;
To see the bees in their luxurious quest
    From bloom to bloom with busy ardor fly,
    While mother-birds, with long-drawn, plaintive
        cry,
Recall the little wanderers to the nest;

To hear the murmer of complaining trees,
    The beat of far-off waves upon the shore,
To feel the light touch of the south wind's kiss,
And look through Nature's eyes, until one sees
    Her myriad timid lives, unknown before,—
Oh, what on earth can be so sweet as this?

The Earth is Our Own

The earth is ours?   Nay, tenants are we all,
  Tenants at will of unrelenting fate;
  Even now, before life's opening outer gate
They stand, to whom the earth full soon will fall.
Theirs are the streams ye drain from fancied
      needs,
  The trees ye fell, and leave a place of death
  Instead of forests with their healing breath,
The falls that vanish to exploit your deeds.
What will ye answer, when of you they ask
  "Where is the beauty which you held in trust?
  What use to us these heaps of golden dust,
With earth a prison where we do our task?"

The Silent Singers

Where are they now, dead singers of dear songs?
  Where are the souls, vibrant with melody,
  Whom sweet sounds sought as waters seek the
      sea,
To whom great thoughts converged in shining
      throngs?
From them seemed lifted Eden's primal curse—
  They talked with angels, and were unafraid;
  Can death destroy those thrilling chords which
      made
Them harps Æolean of the universe ?

When some great star sends down its shining light,

l wonder if they, waiting, learn to know
  The meaning of the planets, as they go·
Singing together on their pathway bright,
And if they come, in visions of the night,
  And chant those wondrous harmonies below.

Regret

When first from thy dear eyes the love-light fled,
  And rigid grew those tender lips, and cold,
  From out my heart arose the cry of old,
"Oh, would that thou had'st lived and I were dead."
But now I bend above thy hidden head
  When night draws near with pomp of rose and
    gold,
  Or breath thy name when Dawn's white lids
    unfold,
And gladness mingles with the tears I shed.

For since for evermore one of us twain
  Must bear Grief's chrism upon an aching brow,
And evermore must listen, but in vain,
  For tones sealed with eternal silence now,
And long for death as misers long for gain,—
  'Tis well, beloved, that 'tis I, not thou.

Fifty Degrees Below Zero

We see the pale, reluctant day appear
  Slowly above the hills that hem us round;
  The small, cold sun is rainbow ringed and bound,
And on each side shines out a sister sphere.
From the deep wells white shafts of vapor rear
  Their misty shapes, in frigid sunlight drowned,
  And the awed ear is startled by the sound
Of bursting tree-trunks, in the forest near.

The brief day passes and gives place to night—
  Night with dark skies, and stars that burn and
    glow,
With triple moons of luminous, clear light,
  Banded with all the hues the prism can show.
Fair lies the world, stilted by the winter's breath—
But 'tis the beauty and the calm of death.

The Empty Nest

To-day I found a little empty nest,
  Fashioned with rarest and most patient skill;
  A few soft, tiny feathers lingered still
Where once reposed the loving mother's breast.
But she will come no more from weary quest
  With food for every tender, open bill;
  No more her care their every want can fill—
They wander far, who once found here their nest.

Ah me, my nest is empty, too, to-day,
  The birdlings whom I loved and reared have
    flown;
The words now left unsaid I cannot say,
  The lessons still unlearned will ne'er be known;
Once on each heart I wrote whate'er I willed,
But ere I knew, the snowy leaves were filled.

To Him Who Hath

Measure me not by what I may achieve,
  Nor mark my progress by the heighth I gain;
  How can you know with what sore heart and
    pain
I strive for that which others but receive?
How can you know how I am weighted down,
  What dead men's sins press heavy on my soul?
  Or how I can but creep toward my goal,
While others pass me, reaching for their crown?

By this, I pray you, mark my onward way—

The daily strife with bonds that hold me fast,
  Like shadowy fingers, reaching from the past,
Holding a token which I must obey;
Pity the fettered feet that but mark time,
  While others march and gain the hills sublime.

The Symphony of Nature

In all the grand procession of the years,
  The seasons with their changes, subtle, sweet,
  The too-brief summer, and the winter's sleet,
My heart has found the chord of bliss and tears.
The brightest hours of all my life were set
  In starry eves, or moonlit summer nights,
  Or sunny days, all filled with dear delights,
Whose passage left me memory and regret.

So when the east is flushed with morning's rose,
  Or in a golden glory dies the day,
The folded leaves of memory unclose,
  And bear me with their magic far away.
With sighing wind and wave I wander free—
The beauty of the earth gives wings to me.

"There's a Joy in the Heart of Pain"

Some day which at the farthest shall be near
  The eyes which meet thy own shall close for aye,
  The hands which clasp thine shall become but
      clay,
And silent be the voices now so dear;
Then shalt thou be thrice blest if they who here
  Walked close beside thee in Life's weary way
  No angry, unkind word e'er heard thee say,
And shed for thee no bitter, hidden tear.

This is the secret of grief's wild unrest,
  Which gives to loneliness its keenest sting—
To know that thou, whose life was crowned and blest
  With that most rare and precious earthly thing,
A heart that loved thee with a true, pure flame,
Knew not its worth—until the angels came!

Thou Hast a Noble Guest, O Flesh

Put by thy weaknesses, O trembling flesh,
   Summon thy will to grapple with thy foes;
   Faint not with terror 'neath the stinging blows
Dealt by the cares which hold thee in their mesh.
Fear this, and only this—that thou should'st fail
   To rise above the littleness of life,
   To gather strength and courage from its strife,
And from its deepest meaning raise the veil.

Forget not that thou hast a noble guest,
   Who from the watch-tower of thy inmost thought
With gladness sees thee in thy upward quest,
   And sorrows when earth's dross thy heart hath
      bought;
This guest, who lifts thee from thy brother clod,
Is co-eternal with Almighty God.

Ante Lucem

If I could know that in some genial clime
   This marred, imperfect life might e'er attain
   The goal toward which I almost hopeless strain,
With patience I should tread the paths of Time.
Now, tortoise-like, through winter's cheerless rime,
   And summer days that seem too fair for pain,
   I onward toil, the heighth afar to gain,
Which seems each day more distant and sublime.

My soul has deeps that never yet were stirred;
   My heart has pulses which have never thrilled;

They wait in vain some magic master-word,—
  Some unknown purpose to be yet fulfilled.
Death, when I meet at last thy dread eclipse,
Be thou to me my soul's apocalypse.

To the Poet

Polish and carve, until thy words shall be
  Like clearest crystal o'er the thought below;
  Like some imprisoned ruby let it glow,
That he who readeth may its beauty see.
'Tis not mere words, though chosen skilfully,
  Which give to verse the witchery we know;
  Like liquid music may sweet numbers flow,
Which pass and die as leaves fall from the tree.

'Tis the strong thought, in fitting words enshrined,
  Shining from out its setting like a star,
Which claims the lasting homage of the mind,
  Recurring oft, through days and scenes afar.
Then, lest thy toil be wasted ere 'tis wrought,
Be sure thy verse reveals a noble thought.

A Winter Morning

The soft, blue sky leaned down toward the earth,
    Veiled with white, fleecy clouds that moved
        and stirred
    Like the light pinions of some sleeping bird,
Poised in the ether where it had its birth.
An opal radiance shimmered in the east,
    Mounted and widened, till, shot through its bars,
    The arrows of the sun dispersed the stars,
Glad from their service to be thus released.
No sun which lights a perfect day in June
    Has ever known a fairer sky than this;
It should be welcomed by the song-birds' tune,
    Its rose and gold should greet the south-wind's
        kiss;
Who could believe, did he not glance below,
This glory bends above a waste of snow?

Night

Who has not felt the beauty of the night,
    The solemn glory of its starlit space?
    Who has not tried, with reverent awe, to trace
The stars which sang in the first morning's light?
Who has not looked, and trembling, felt His might
    Who gives to worlds their own appointed place,
    And yet who watches, with omniscient grace,
Each human atom on these planets bright?
And sometimes, picturing that fair world whose
    bliss

And grandeur far transcends our highest thought,
We seek with earth-held eyes a type in this,
And wonder what more glorious God hath wrought,
Since we are told that heaven's clear skies will
      miss
The revelation which our evening brought.

Exploration

I need not seek the Pole's eternal snows
    To learn their wondrous, silent mystery;
    Each year the Arctic hither comes to me,
Bringing the weird Aurora's changing rose,
Dark skies, in which each planet burns and glows,
    Gray dawns, which scarce reveal gray land and
      sea,
    And noons more drear than night itself can be,
With chilling winds, which beat with cruel blows.

Here, too, I know the ardent Tropic's zone;
    Long days, which melt to nights of argent flame;
    Lush grasses hiding life unseen, unknown,
And flying winds, too swift, too light, for name.
For me the winter wanes and summer dies,
    A traveller whose anchors never rise.

Alone

Alone each soul must journey o'er the way
  Which leads to realms where silence reigns
      supreme;
  There is no speech of souls, save thoughts which
      gleam
From the dear eyes whose lovelight makes our
      day;
Words are so impotent, they oft betray
  The heart which trusts them with its dearest
      theme.
Lives touch our own, and we perhaps may dream
That love can see beyond the walls of clay,
  But when God calls "Where art thou?" and we
      stand
  With souls uncovered, shrinking from the gaze
Of purity unveiled, would one whose hand
  We clasped on earth, still know us in that blaze?
Alone we hither came—from what far strand?
Alone we shall depart, to death's strange land.

The Song Which Lives

Of war and honor, love and death, they sang—
The bards, who lived in far, heroic times;
They sought no quaint conceits or sounding rymes,
But life's great passions through their measures
      rang.
So Helen lives, and still we hear the clang
Of shield and spear beneath the walls of Troy;
We see Penelope her arts employ,
And feel poor Hero's utmost fear and pang.
But they who sing to-day—save he whose word
Measures our heartbeats, and whose pen is fire,
The "Friend of all the World"—what heart is
      stirred
By their sweet strains, which gracefully expire?
Singers arise and with their lays depart—
The song which lives is written with the heart.

The Deserted Farmhouse

Set in green fields, far from the narrow way, '
    Stood an old farmhouse, with its windows bare;
    No smoke rose curling on the morning air—
Chilly it looked, although the time was May.
It seemed to miss the children, who in play
    Once sang and shouted, free from fear or care,
    Around its high-silled doors; no life was there,
Even the pasture green and empty lay.

From the great barn no placid cows looked out,
    Or drank from the clear brook that rippled by;
    No bees hummed in the weather-beaten hive;
No lonelier is Pompeii, walled about
    With drifts volcanic, shutting out the sky,
    A tomb of those who filled it when alive.

On the Western Slope

The traveler where Life's rough pathways wind
    Knows not when he has passed the mountain
        crest,
    Until he finds his road turned toward the West,
And looking back, he sees the height behind.
Yet for awhile, how gentle is the slope,
    How light his burden—for he still must bear
    His weight of sorrow, poverty,. or care—
And still he sees his gentle comrade, Hope.

But soon, ah, soon, the way grows rough and. hard;
    The sky grows dark, for night is drawing near;

No, more sweet Hope is nigh, to whisper cheer,
His feet are bruised with stones and broken shard.
  The pathway ends above a gulf unknown;
  He can but leap—and he must go alone.

What Freedom Cost

Ye silent men, who to your country gave
  That last full measure of devotion—life—
  Ye fell asleep while the tumultuous strife
Around you swelled in fury like the wave
Which breaks upon the rocks that prove its grave.
  To-day, around you all the air is rife
  With wailing cries from bugle and from fife,
The voice of that dear land you tried to save.

Nay, ye have never died! Ye live to-day
In that fair flag with which the breezes play,
  With every flashing star undimmed, unlost;
In every soul which joys that it is free,
In every heart, which clay like yours shall be,
  Before our land forgets what freedom cost.

The Proof of Love

Not in the calm content of peaceful hours,
　Is Love, the conqueror and master, proved;
　Who knew, while evenly life's current moved,
How strong might be the bond of clasping flowers?
Nor may the winds of circumstance, that sweep,
　Like chaff, all power and garnered wealth away,
　Alone prove Love, that in thy heart holds sway,
So thou shalt know if it be true and deep.

But by this test Love's purity is shown;
　If in companionship's clear light, which bares
Each hidden weakness, to the world unknown,
Thou shalt forgive each, as thou dost thine own,
　And feel the pity which a mother shares,
　Then hast thou known the Love which lives and
　　　dares.

A Winter Sunset

Based on the dazzling whiteness of the snow
　Arose fair towers, crimson and tipped with gold,
　From which unrolled brave pennants, fold on
　　　fold,
Waving defiance to an unseen foe.
The night crept on—the crescent moon rode high,
　Attended by her lonely, faithful star;
　The shadows deepened—but still stood afar
That pillared wonder in the glowing sky.

Long, long it lingered, till the last faint gleam

Of day slipped softly down the western stair;
Then every cloud, awaking from its dream, ˙
   Gave up each picture it had prisoned there.
The banners drooped—down fell the lofty towers—
Night reigned unchallenged o'er this world of ours.

The Land of Dream

Midnight is here, and earth is wrapped in sleep;
   I only, of all near me, watch and wake;
   All others to that land the pathway take,
Where dreams their tantalizing promise keep.
There are no hearts that ache, no eyes that weep;
   The rose of health blooms brightly on each
      cheek;
   Voices long silent in sweet converse speak,
And long closed eyes meet ours with glances deep.

O, Land of Dreams! O, pleasant Land of Dreams!
   Where reason dwells not, with unpitying light,
   Where time stands still, nor leaves its cruel blight,
Where hearts are true, and all is what it seems.
   In your enchanted realm I live again—
   Here, I but dream—amid the haunts of men !

Autumn

When first the hand of Spring unlocks the showers
   And sets the prisoned buds and grasses free,
   We say, "How beautiful the world will be
When June comes with her crown of royal flowers."
But when at last we see the rose-wreathed bowers,
   And hear the bobolink's ecstatic glee,
   We lightly hold the beauty which we see,
And dream of fairer and more perfect hours.

Until some day we hear with tender ruth
   The crickets chirping in some creviced stone;
Ah, so we lightly spill the wine of youth,
   And idly dream of roses still unblown,
But suddenly awake to know the truth—
   The June of life, with all its flowers, has flown.

Lincoln

On history's white page he stands alone—
   Our Lincoln, with his martyr's aureole crowned;
   He sought not fame, and yet her plaudits drowned
Detraction's clamor and hate's undertone.
A noble soul from every feature shown,
   Stern, rugged, in the mills of effort ground
   To symmetry; his life-horizon's bound
Was faith in God, and trust for all unknown.

A man was he of nature's finest clay,
   Born with the strength to climb, the power to rule;
Sad with the sadness great minds know alway,

He played with mirth, and used it for a tool.
Through him we have a land made one and free—
After such toil, how welcome rest must be!

Opportunity

This is the sharpest pang which failure brings,
   To know that sweet success was near, so near,
   We missed it only by a hairbreadth here;
Or, idly musing over meaner things,
Sought not occasion, till it used its wings.
   Alas! for though delusive hope may cheer
   Our hearts awhile with songs both sweet and
      clear,

Yet shall we learn that fate but one time flings
   Open the door of opportunity,
That each may enter and his guerdon win.
   None pass it ever with impunity—
Its triple bolts move only from within.
   Nor prayer nor tear avails—we wander evermore
   Like shipwrecked sailors on an alien shore.

December

Again the great clock in the hall of Time
  Proclaims the midnight of the waning year;
  Again the frozen earth lies brown and sere,
Hidden beneath its winding-sheet of rime.
The budding beauty of the tender Spring,
  The golden promise of the Summer days,
  Autumn's fulfilment—all have gone their ways,
And Winter reigns—dread desolation's king.

He who first saw the passing of the year—
  The trees all bare, the velvet grass all dead,
  The soft earth changed to rock beneath his
      tread—
How could he live through all those days of fear?
  Even we who know, how gladly we shall see
  The earth unchained, the rivers running free.

"The Centuries Fall Like Grains of Sand"

Sometimes I watch the passing of the sun,
　　While rose and purple splendors veil his car,
　　Or see the moon with her attendant star
Rise o'er earth's rim, her nightly race begun,
Or see the storm clouds gather low and dun,
　　With vivid lightnings darting near and far,
　　While the white waves against the harbor bar
Leap up, like dogs upon the quarry won.

A cycle hence, across you azure arch
　　Sun, moon and stars will pass, and clouds shall be;
Deep unto deep will call its hosts to march
　　Against the land, whose borders mock the sea;
And I—Ah, I shall see it not—that day
I shall be dust beneath some mound of clay.

The Dawning Day

How slow the dawn comes to the eyes that wake;
　　How long her chariot lingers on the hills
　　Before she finds the little, hidden rills,
And glory flashes from the waiting lake.
How long, from every nest on bush and tree,
　　Impatient murmurs from each nestling rise,
　　Before day's flame lights up the morning skies,
And wings released flash upward, glad and free.

How long the pale moon lingers in the west,
　　Guarding the portals of the realm of night,
Before the eager sun begins his eager quest,

And men awake to life, and life's delight,
And ·they who sought. sweet sleep and rest in vain,
May in day's busy hours forget their pain.

Thought

Great thoughts are shy.   Oft in some lonely hour,
   Watching the solemn sky and glorious sun,
   I feel a thrill through all my being run,
As one reveals to me its mighty power.
But ere slow speech can seize it, it has fled,
   Like fantasies of sleep from morning's light,
   And though I sorrowing search, and long invite,
It comes no more—my wondrous thought is dead.

Or if sometimes I warily am still,
   Until soft plumage nestles on my heart,
And close I clasp it, with caressing art,
   To find it mine, surrendered to my will,
Behold, the iridescent light is gone;
The glory vanished, though the thought lives on.

Threnody

The saddest thing in all the world is this:
   The emerald of the springing grass to see,
   The tender leaves come forth on bush and tree,
And hear the birds pour out their hearts in bliss;
To find in dimpled dells which winters miss,
   The violets blooming, fair and sweet and free,
   To feel your whole soul thrill in ecstasy
Beneath the syren south wind's perfumed kiss;

And yet to know that when your loving eyes
   Are closed beneath the low-arched roof of mould,
Sweet birds will sing, warm suns set and arise,
   And soft, slow winds will wander, as of old,
Nor pause one moment by the mound where lies
   The heart which loved them—hidden now and
      cold!

June

Here summer halts upon her Northward way,
   And drops the flowery burden which she brought
   From tropic lands, with fragile beauty wrought,
And dyed with hues like sunset clouds astray.
Now night glides softly into perfect day,
   And waning day is merged in fairest night;
   Soft smiles the sun through drifts of fleecy white,
And laughing Southern breezes hither stray.

This is the climax of the perfect year,
   And if we had no other joy but this—
   To feel the sunshine's soft, pervading bliss,
   To see and know the beauty of the earth,
The calm, blue skies and waters deep and clear—
   Oh, life were still a gift of heavenly birth.

New England

There is a land which the Atlantic laves,
   A land of groves, and fields, and purling rills;
   Fair are its storied vales and noble hills,
And grand the voices of wind-driven waves.
It is the land which holds our fathers' graves,
   Although the fields they trod another tills;
   Its beauty all our childhood's memory fills,
And oft the heart its peace and quiet craves.

It is the granary which held Freedom's seed
   Secure through war, and more insidious peace,
Till, scattered far, when rose the time of need

It wrought the land's redemption and release.
New England!   Mother of a nation free!
The Occident gives greeting unto thee.

The Sphinx on the Hearth

No need have I to seek the sphinx afar—
  She lies with bended elbows on my knee;
  Her gleaming amber eyes are turned on me,
Remote and passionless as some fixed star.
Yet anger, love, devotion unto death,
  And courage high, her timid spirit knows;
  Though sleeping now, within her bosom glows
The same hot fires fanned by our human breath.

Gentle, yet tameless, all our life she shares,
  Yet lives her own, with joys and fears apart;
Once worshipped, still a regal mien she wears,
  And claims the homage of each tender heart.
Behind those eyes inscrutable if I might see,
Should I not find close kinship unto me?

The Voice of the Deep

Sometimes I weary of the puny race
  Which launches fragile craft upon my breast,
  In which to sail upon some trifling quest,
And thinks me tamed when I but give it grace.
On every sea men dare my might and wrath;
  Even my Arctic fastness they invade;
  Ah, how their souls faint in them, sore afraid,
When I rise to sweep them from my path.

Not all the forces of the earth, unchained,
  Can wreak the vengeance which I hold in store,
  When from my fetters I am freed once more,
And find my ancient kingdom all regained;
  Only His power, who holds me in His hand,
  Saves from my fury, day by day, the land.

Beyond the Bar

Once all the winds that blew had calls for me,
  And brought me messages from lands afar;
  Once in the radiance of each brilliant star
I found companionship, not mystery.
But since she launched upon an unknown sea,
  Where none may know where any harbors are
  And each frail boat may wreck on unseen bar,
The universe is filled with awe for me.

For since I, too, full soon must sail away
  Upon that chartless and unharbored sea,
How shall I pass, through tides that swell and sway,

To that far orb from whence she watches me?
For well I know that she is waiting there—
That sweet, white soul, who must make heaven
    more fair.

The Gods of Old

And Moses was a hundred and twenty years old when he died; his eye was not dimmed, nor his natural force abated.

I know whence came the old, immortal tales
  Of Gods who feared not age, nor time's decay;
  It was life's protest, in that earlier day,
Against the coward flesh which shrinks and fails.
In vain the soul's command, the will's decree,
  Some time the body will refuse its aid,
  The purpose high by weakness be betrayed,
And night close down, while still the eyes can see.

Well might they call them gods, who knew not this,
  Who felt not, while life's tide leaped full and high,
  A foe within—insiduous, lurking nigh,
Waiting to taint the deepest draught of bliss.
  Well might they call them gods, whom age
    passed by,
Whose strength failed not, who only had to die.

PATRIOTIC POEMS

Come Gather Today

Come, gather to-day from the hill and the plain,
Leave your life's daily toil and planning for gain;
Come hither, with all that is fairest and best
To lay on the graves of our heroes at rest;
Our heroes—above whose low dwellings to-day
A nation has gathered, its tribute to pay.
Bring music, and song, and the fairest of flowers
From the garden and field, and the dim woodland
      bowers,
For the graves that we garland the altar shall be
Where our vows we renew o'er the dust of the free.
All over our land they are lying asleep;
By the ocean, whose waves still their sad vigil keep,
By the lovely Potomac, whose blue, sunny wave
So often was red with the blood of the brave,
By the mountains, where Kenesaw guarded the glen
When Sherman marched by with his legions of men,
Or Lookout, whose cloud-enwreathed summit one
      day
Saw a battle where blood ran like wine in the fray.
From the homes which they loved their graves
      lie afar,
Who died that our banner might miss not one star.
Where the shadows of battle fell darkly and chill
Stand the cities of Silence, all mutely and still;
No sentinel guards the cold, white-gleaming stone;
The soldier, unarmed, lies there helpless and prone,
Still robed in the blue which he honored so well,

For he fell where he fought, and he rests where
      he fell.
We know of the spirit so valiant and brave
Whose glory sank down in the gloom of the grave,
But never a mortal can measure or know
What joys of the living lie buried below.
Alas, for the hopes which had bloomed through
      the years,
But faded and died in that tempest of tears.
There's many a mother who knows not what grave
Hides the face of her first born, his hair's sunny
      wave,
And many a wife who knows not to-day
Where her hero is sleeping the glad years away.
Oh, the dreams they had dreamed of a future so fair,
Which they who are sleeping should bless and
      should share;
But the sun of their joy set in darkness and tears,
And the shadows grow deeper, through all the
      long years.
When the echoes of cannon from Sumpter were
      heard,
Into line sprang our soldiers, nor waited a word;
Sad farewells were spoken, and prayers softly said,
When they left us to swell the long ranks of the dead.
Oh, little we knew, as they marched on their way,
Where their pathway would lead, or how long they
      would stay.
Beside them marched spectres like demons
      uncaged,

Grim famine, and fever, and murder enraged;
The red fields of battle lay thick in their way,
And the unbuilded prison awaited its prey;
But their eyes were holden—they knew not their
     doom,
Nor knew that they marched toward a wide-open
     tomb.
They dreamed of the time when with beat of the
     drum
And clamor of fife, they should conquerors come;
When their names through the homes of their
     childhood should ring,
And bards tell their deeds in the songs they should
     sing;
When the country they rescued should greet them
     with cheers,
And the eyes that they loved should brim over
     with tears—
Tears of joy and of pride—alas, they were shed
O'er names in the lists of the missing and dead.
O silent Grand Army! Our pulses may thrill
When we tell of your deeds—yours are bloodless
     and still;
Not even the garlands we bring you today
Can move the strong arms that are folded for aye;
The bugle's loud blare and the drum's muffled beat
Cannot pierce the sealed ear nor move the stilled
     feet;
Not even the voice of our country could stir

The heart which once throbbed with devotion
    for her.
We honor not you, O dead heroes, today,
But ourselves, when our laurels above you we lay,
For your names will grow brighter with luster untold
When the wreaths that we bring you are turned
    into mould;
And we claim you and mourn you, O soldiers, as ours,
And the voice of our love is these beautiful flowers.
Till the last roll is called, and we all answer "Here,"
We will garland your graves in the morn of the year,
And each flower that we gather with reverent thought
Is an oath to remember the deeds you have wrought,
Deeds which will live till remembrance shall cease,
And bourgeon and bloom into ages of peace!

May 30

In a long past May the drums were beating,
  And the notes of the fife grew shrill with ire,
Long grew the lines of soldiers meeting,
  And the land was filled with battle fire.
Up from the south came the cannon's thunder,
  And hearts at home grew faint with fear
Till the clouds of war were rent asunder,
  And the sun of Peace shone bright and clear.
Oh, little we heeded the May-time splendor
  As we watched the soldiers march away—
There was manhood stern and boyhood tender,
  And each was eager for the fray.
Ah, many a foot went marching gaily
  Which came not back when the war was done,
And our ears were filled with the moaning daily
  Of the mother weeping for her son,
The stricken maid for her plighted lover,
  The lonely wife for her husband slain,
And still the heavy cloud hung over,
  And the whole land seemed a battle plain.
Back they came with the strong ranks broken—
  Many tney went, but few they came—
And the tale of their daring deeds unspoken
  Was traced on each brow in battle flame.
Stern were the lips that once smiled brightly,
  Erect and firm was the measured tread,
Steady the eyes that once roved lightly,
  Somber with thought of a comrade dead;

Back they came with their banner flying,
　　With no star lost or its glory dim,
And the sound of the wives and mothers crying
　　Was drowned in a great triumphal hymn.
O land of our love, of our heart's devotion,
　　With a heavy price was your glory bought,
For from eastern sea to western ocean
　　Close lie the graves of men who fought.
Some lives went out on the field of glory,
　　Some in the prison pen alone,
But each name shall live in his country's story
　　Till the stars from her flag fade out unknown.
But the swift years gather and wait behind us,
　　And the blue-clad lines grow thin and slow,
And the Day of the Dead, as it comes to find us,
　　Sees gaps in the ranks it used to know.
Men of the line once full and steady,
　　Whose souls are strong and whose hears are true,
Whose lives were laid on the altar ready,
　　Till your country gave them back to you,
When you meet around your comrades sleeping,
　　Furloughed forever from pain and care,
What does it mean to you, when you are keeping
　　This tryst with the dead which we see and share?
Do the muffled drum with its voices hollow
　　And the drooping flag which you bear to-day
Speak to your hearts of their love who follow
　　Your steps to the tents where your comrades
　　　　stay ?

Do you know that the world still looks with wonder
 At the fields you won, when your foes you met
In the wild,. swift charge to the cannon's thunder,
 With the unsheathed saber and bayonet?
Ah, it seems but a dream of the past—the marches
 With the foe behind and the foe before,
Where the southern pine with its shade o'erarches,
 And the river dips to the warm gulf shore.
No more shall the noon-day, fierce and burning,
 With its sudden storms o'ercloud your sky;
You stand with your face to the sunset turning,
 And shadows soft in your pathway lie.
March on—till you come to the shadowy valley
 Where the sentry Death shall bid you stand,
Where the Great Commander your lines shall rally,
 With your long lost comrades on either hand.

Memorial Day

Soldiers of the Silent Army! You whose half-told
 days shall shine .
On the calendar of ages with a radiance divine,
You whose memory is the anchor of our country's
 . ˙ storm-tossed bark,
Binding her to truth and freedom when the skies
 are veiled and dark,
You whose sightless eyes behold us, and whose
 shadowy forms are near,
Rouse your spirits from their slumbers, and our

heartfelt pledges hear!
By the sky that arches o'er us, bright with Summer's loveliest blue,   .
By the garlands that we bring you, smiling through
    their tears of dew,
By each fond remembrance clinging to the earthly
    forms you wore,
By each heart that broke with anguish, when you
    fell to rise no more,
By each hope that faded with you from love's
    shining morning sky,
By each life whose joy departed when you laid you
    down to die,
By the banner that you gave us, free from every
    spot and stain,
Never, while the crimson life-blood courses swiftly
    through each vein,
Shall the land which you enfranchised bear a tyrant
    or a slave,
While its soil supports a footstep, or its depths
    afford a grave.

Our Flag

Float out, O starry banner, to every wind that blows,
Earth's peerless flower of beauty, Freedom's con-
    stellate rose !
When first thy thirteen planets flamed out upon
    the sky
How little dreamed this nation how far those folds
    would fly;
Unknown upon the waters, despised upon the
    strand,
No seer foretold thy glory, O emblem of our land!
How many men have perished, on mountain, shore
    and sea,
How many women's hearts have bled, only for
    love of thee !
The stars upon thy azure field have gleamed
    through battle years,
Thy stripes are red with precious blood, or white
    with rain of tears;
And sheltered 'neath thy spreading folds, which
    glow with heaven's own light,
Are all dear things that earth can give and all that
    makes life bright;
Like him of old, we vow to-day, from ocean shore
    to shore,
To serve thee with our fortunes, lives, and honor,
    evermore!

The Price of Freedom

Freedom is never lightly won,
　　Her price is blood, and pain, and tears;
They by whose hands the work is done
　　Must leave its gains for happier years.
The height they saw, with upraised eyes,
　　Shall be the path their children tread;
And all they dared to win the prize,
　　Earth shall not know till they are dead.

But though death's flames leap high and roll
　　Across the path of Freedom's shore,
Earth shall not lack the patriot soul
　　Till tyranny shall be no more.

The Reunion of the G. A. R.

Close up!　The lines are lessening fast,
The blasts of death are sweeping past,
And he who missed us on the field,
Where shot and shell his track revealed,
With silent tread is stealing on;
Our ranks are thinned; our comrades gone;
No bugle call will sound retreat,
We onward move, our foes to greet.
Close up!　Close up!　Then—forward march!
Each year sees thousands lying low,
And we who stay have steps more slow;
The frosts of time have touched each head,
Our speech is grave, our jests all sped.

Still facing front, unconquered, brave,
We rally where our guidons wave,
Knowing that soon we all shall hear
The signal, sounding loud and clear,
Put out the lights!   Put out the lights!

The Banner of Song and of Story

What flower of the air above us is flying,
In the sunshine displaying each glorious hue?
Like the stars of the night are the stars on it lying,
Like the azure above is its beautiful blue.
'Tis the emblem of freedom the ages have sighed for,
The freedom which patriots have fought and have
died for;
'Tis the standard our forefathers bravely defended,
The flag without stain, which to us has descended;
'Tis the flag of our country. unmatched in its glory,
'Tis the Star Spangled Banner of song and of story.

Closed are the eyes that first flashed at its glory,
Dust are the feet that first answered its call;
The voices are silent that first sung its story,
And bade us defend it, whatever befall.
Only with death shall our faithful hands leave it,
Until death guard it well, O ye who receive it!
Let shame and dishonor abide near it never,
And no foe shall withstand it, unconquered forever;
And the Star Spangled Banner of song and of story
Shall float on through the ages, unmatched in its glory.

Peace, or War?

'Tis well to keep the truce of Peace
   And leave the sword undrawn,
For well we know that woe must come
   When red War walks at dawn.

Tarry before ye sound the drum
   To wake the call to arms,
For in War's train shall evil creep,
   And work a thousand harms.

But mark ye this—till time shall cease,
   The hand in mail shall be
The keeper of the Nation's rights
   And hopes of liberty;

And when oppression stalks abroad
   Earth's best-beloved is he
Who bares his sword and stakes his life
   To keep his country free.

Gone into Camp

Thin are the blue-clad ranks to-day, once half a
million strong,
And slow and feeble are the feet that once marched
far long;
Once more together they will march with slow,
uncertain tramp,
To see their comrades who have gone before them
into camp.

The tents are spread—the low, green tents, whose
curtains tightly close;
No reveille will waken those who sweetly here
repose;
No more their weary feet will toil o'er highways
rough and damp—
For them the long, hard march is done, for they've
gone into camp.

Their comrades come with songs and flowers; the
banner of their love
Floats proudly out upon the air, their low, close
tents above;
Ah, many a mile they followed it with strong and
steady tramp,
Before they heard the order given—"Break ranks
—go into camp."

Soon all the weary feet will halt, the last march
will be made,
For them the low, green tents be spread on hillside

or in glade;
No more together will they march with slow and
　　broken tramp—
To all the order will be given—"Break ranks—go
　　into camp."

Memorial Day Remembrances

In the morning of my life-time, many long, long
　　years ago,
When within our country's borders brothers met
　　a brother foe,
When the earth was glad with sunshine and May
　　sweetness filled the air,
Once with others I stood waiting—waiting by the
　　roadside bare.
Soon the throbbing air was vibrant with the noise
　　of drum and fife,
And we saw the blue-clad soldiers marching to the
　　field of strife;
O, I see them still so plainly—see again each
　　white, set face—
Then the noise grew faint and distant, and they
　　left but empty space.
O, the many who went marching far away toward
　　the South,
O, the few who came back to us, each with grave
　　and firm-set mouth,
Each with eyes that told the story of the vision
　　they had seen—

Pale death riding on the whirlwind, hurling arrows
    swift and keen;
Through the years whose ghosts pursue us from
    the dim and shadowy past
They have lived and moved among us, with
    whose lot their own is cast;
But whenever May comes to us, bringing flowers
    and skies of blue,
Once again the spell is on them, and their youth-
    time they renew.

Once again they march together to the sound of
    fife and drum,
But they hear no bellowing cannon hoarsely call-
    ing them to come;
Hosts in arms no more await them, bullets stop
    no more the way,
But they march beneath their banner as they
    marched that sweet May day.
Ah, for them no more forever shall the wine of
    battle flow,
Never shall men hail them victor, while the clang-
    ing trumpets blow.
Year by year they march together to the field
    where each shall know
At the last—defeat and silence, when their con-
    queror lays them low.
See, they seek their fallen comrades, sleeping with
    . untroubled breasts,
Keeping 'neath their green tents ever the unbroken

truce of rest.
Let no tear-drop dim the glory of one aureole-
 circled grave—
They have done with grief and weeping—bring
 no sorrow to the brave;
Bring them evergreen and laurel, emblems of the
 matchless fame
Which they won while death pursued them,
 wrapped in sheets of blinding flame;
Bring them pansies, for remembrance of their cour-
 age true and high,
Roses for the love and gladness which beneath
 their tombstones lie;
Lillies for the white souls offered on the altar of
 our land,
Till their red blood quenched the bale-fire, by the
 breath of warfare fanned.
Rest in peace, ye dead, forever! to the utmost
 bounds of time
Shall your deeds be told in story, sung in poet's
 proudest rhyme;
And whenever May-flowers blossom, like fair
 jewels on earth's breast,
Shall the hands of freemen wreath them round the
 green beds where ye rest.

The Oregon

Turn back thy prow, O Oregon,
　Toward thy western home;
No foeman's ship will bar thy way,
　Or cross thy track of foam;
By day, by night, like hounds in leash,
　No more thy engines strain
To reach the sepulcher where sleeps
　Thy sister ship, the Maine.
O, nobly thou hast played thy part—
　Though half the world away,
Like arrow to its mark ye sped,
·　To join and win the fray.
Go back, O Oregon, in peace!
　'Mid wondrous deeds and bold
Thy rush of fourteen thousand miles
　Shall ever more be told.

Keenan's Charge at Chancellorsville

Oh, tell not of Leonidas and the pass he guarded
　well,
Where with his brave three hundred so long ago
　he fell;
Why search through misty ages for deeds of dar-
　ing high?
The men who charged with Keenan have taught
　us how to die.

Through every vein the life blood pulsed with

rythmic ebb and flow,
Before them stretched the happy years, illumed
    by hope's bright glow,
Yet with one breath life's noon-day sun was
    stricken from their sky—
Think you they heard unmoved the word which
    doomed them then to die?

Theirs not the hope even valor craves—to win the
    hard-fought fray;
Knowing their graves before them yawned, they
    sped along the way;
No faltering hand a charger checked, although full
    well they knew
With every step their life's short span of seconds
    shorter grew.

Sleep sweetly, O ye heroes! When English bards
    shall tell
How Nolan and his soldiers at Balaklava fell,
We'll show them where you charged alone an
    army on its way,
And say, "Here died their brothers—as true, as
    brave as they."

Memorial Day

Blossom, O flowers, in riotous splender!
  Open, O lingering buds, to the light!
I will gather you all, fresh, fragrant and tender,

And weave you in garlands, sweet, dewy and
    bright.
Over the graves where our heroes are sleeping
    I will lay all your beauty and innocent bloom,
That they o'er whose dust a proud nation is weeping
    May know that we love them, though low in the
    tomb.

What are our wreaths to the garlands they offered
    On liberty's altars—the white flowers of life?
What are our tears to the red drops they proffered—
    The warm blood that flowed o'er the hot flames
    of strife?
All we can give of remembrance most tender
    Is but a leaf in the crown of the brave,
Or drops which, illumined by his glory's bright
    splendor,
    Will change to an aureole over his grave.

O for the tones that are silent forever;
    O for the hearts that were true to the right;
O for the arms that knew weariness never,
    But fought all the day till death's swift-falling
    night.
Nothing but freedom is worth such devotion;
    Only the land which our forefathers gave,
Redeemed and unbroken from ocean to ocean,
    Is worth half the cost of one soldier's low grave.

War Voices

Hark, the drum calls "Follow, follow"
With reverberation hollow,
And the fife screams, "Hither, come,
I am brother of the drum;
And we call you, call you hither;
Follow us and ask not whither."

Then the bugle shrieks "Obey me,
Follow, follow, nor delay me,
Follow us the wide world over
Where the clouds of battle hover,
Leaving father, mother, lover;
Though at first your heart shall sicken,
When you see the red blood thicken,
You shall laugh to see it flowing,
On the trampled greensward growing.
War, hell's eldest, dearest daughter,
Bids you follow to the slaughter."

"Come," the bugle shrieks, "obey me,
Follow, follow, nor delay me;"
And the fife screams, "Hither, hither,
Follow, follow, ask not whither."
And the loud, compelling drum
Echoes, "Follow, follow, come."

The Sleeping Brave

Men from whose lifted hand
  Once dropped the tool or pen
At Duty's stern command,
  Oh, rouse ye once again.

Take ye these lovely flowers
  From garden and from grove,
Children of sun and showers,
  Full-freighted with our love.

For you we dare not weep,
  Nor for your half-told days;
The bed where heroes sleep
  Is warmed by Glory's blaze.

We count not freedom's cost
  Of manhood or of youth,
But mourn that earth has lost
  So much of strength and truth.

LATER POEMS

The Lords of Life and Love and Death

Three wanderers passed my humble door:
  Stately, and strong and fair were they;
  One moved untrammeled on his way,
And two a heavy burden bore.

Behind one, flowers sprang from the plain,
  And song birds circled where he stood,
  And when he looked at me, the blood
Went singing, surging through each vein.

"Who art thou, lord?"   To fear was vain,
  For even his look with joy was fraught;
  "My name is Life, and I have brought
Thy heritage of bliss and pain."

Light seemed the burden which I felt;
  Then to my side another drew,
  Crowned with fair heartsease and with rue,
And silent at his feet I knelt.

"A heavy burden thou must bear,
  For thou art woman, I am Love—
  And Love and Life thy strength shall prove,
For Love shall all thy being share."

A great bliss swept me like a wave;
  A great grief filled me, and I wept;
  I bowed where his light feet had stept,
And said, "Have pity on thy slave.

"Lord of us all, I own thy reign—
   But give me peace, and make me blest;
   Take from my heart this wild unrest—
Give me thy joy, and still my pain."

"Nay," said the other, who drew near,
   "That is my gift, and mine alone;
   I lift the burdens thou hast known,
I give thee peace, and take thy fear.

"When Love and Life have lost their spell,
   My love and peace shall comfort thee."
   His noble face looked down on me
And a great calm upon me fell.

The lords of Life and Love and Death
   Passed on and left me where I stood;
   But now a strange, tumultuous flood
Beat in each pulse and moved each breath.

And evermore my doom shall be
   This burden and unrest alway;
   And when they pass from me, that day
Lord Death shall soothe and comfort me.

Man, The Destroyer

By the work of His hand God made them, and he
    pronounced them good—
Creatures of fen and forest, creatures of wold and
    wood,
Each with his plane of living, the river, the land,
    the sea,
And each with the breath in his nostrils which the
    same God gave to thee.
Life and the joy of living—pain and the fear of
    death—
This he gave them for birthright, this they drew in
    with their breath;
Brothers are they—do you feel it when you shoot
    the bird on her nest,
And the seal with the white milk oozing from out
    her wounded breast?
What thinks the kind Lord of you, striving to learn
    His trade,
Wrenching and tearing asunder the nerves and
    the threws He made?
Will the thought of the lives you have taken and
    the pain you have given oft
Brighten the gloom of your death-day, or make
    your death-bed soft?
They are heirs of the earth as you are, with
    strength and courage, yet
What chance have they with the coward trap and
    the lying lure you set?

Think you their Maker hears not the cry they raise
    to Him
When you bind His helpless creatures and tear
    them limb from limb?
You may prate of your skill and science, but be-
    neath your fair white skin
You are the world's Apaches—to the savage alone
    are you kin.

All Passes

Who cometh from the mountains bare and brown?
    Who rises from the somber-shadowed sea?
"I am the spirit of thy joy and hope—"
    "And I bring woe to thee."

"Twin-born, for ages this has been our task—
    To wait upon each year, until its close."
One in its hand held rue of pain and grief,
    The other, joy's red rose.

Full oft their noiseless feet had crossed my path,
    Full oft each tone and face had greeted me;
Oft had I fled from grief's dark-visaged face,
    And turned his twin to see.

I thought I knew them well—that woe or joy
    Must ever bear the look with which he came;
But as I gazed, alike they grew—they smiled—
    Behold! they were the same.

The Days of Old

O days of old, forever past, what is the charm you
　　hold
Which turns your sorrow into joy, your silver into
　　gold?
Oft times your sky was overcast, fierce storms
　　swept o'er your way,
But with a pang of keen regret we think of you
　　today.
Ah me! It was the promise of young life's morn-
　　ing hours,
The glamour of Hope's magic spell which paved
　　the way with flowers;
She showed us all the bliss of earth—it seemed
　　within our grasp—
Alas! It turned to worthless dross when held
　　with eager clasp.
Life's path has wider, smoother grown, the winds
　　are soft and sweet
Which gently touch the fading cheek, as day and
　　twilight meet,
But oh, to know one hour again when all that life
　　can give
Seemed waiting for our hand to take, and it was
　　joy to live!

April

Ring out, O gladsome Easter bells, .
  Your tale of joy to men!
From out the winter's grave of cold
  Earth wakes to life again.
Each bird that from the southward comes
  On pinions swift and strong,
Each flower that blooms from roots that slept
  Where winter lingered long,
Renews a yearly miracle,
  Greater than pen or paint
E'er told in book or pictured scene
  Of wonder-working saint!

A Fragment

When some sweet hope, whose light seemed pure
        and holy,
Which long had blessed my pathway rough and
        lowly,
Has sunk below my soul's horizon slowly,
I oft have said, in vain is all endeavor,
Since joy and peace elude my grasp forever,
While those obtain them who have sought them
        never.
But when the years have made my vision clearer,
I oft have found some bliss which I held dearer,
Which my lost hope, expiring, brought me nearer.

Summer

Velvet turf and turquoise sky,   .
Bird and bee and butterfly;
South wind with the trees at play—
Life is bliss alone today !
While the katydid complains,
While the rainbow follows rains,
While the stars press one by one
On the pathway of the sun
And all night their radiance give,
It is only joy to live !

When Night Has Come

The day grows old, the night falls dark and dreary,
The stars are hid, the wind sounds chill and eerie;
The tired lids droop o'er eyes with slumber weary—
    The Night has come.

Kind Night, which sets a bound to all endeavor,
Which brings us rest and peace and comfort ever,
And sleep, whose gentle benediction fails us never—
    The Night has come.

Rest in her calm, O hearts grown faint with aching,
Take ye her comfort, souls with sorrow aching;
Some time you shall know peace without awaking—
    When Night has come.

The Fathers Have Eaten Sour Grapes

There is a road, weary and long,
   Treeless, windswept and bare;
No happy groups upon it throng—
   Alone I travel there.

Paths wind beside, where grasses grow,
   Whose travelers bear no load;
They are the fields I love and know—
   I never leave the road.

Sometimes when stones have bruised my feet,
   And steep the hills I pass,
I look at the paths so cool, so sweet,
   And long for the smooth, soft grass.

But though for fairer ways I yearn,
   And none my steps would stay,
My very feet refuse to turn,
   And keep the bare, hard way.

My fathers made this path my own—
   They chose this road for me;
It must be mine, to keep alone,
   Until Eternity.

The Silent Harp

The great harp of the world in silence lies,
   While years pass by, with swift, unhurrying wings;
   Since he who sang The Idylls of the King,
No one has claimed it as a rightful prize.

Sometimes a hand has raised it, and has stirred
   The silent strings with murmurs soft and sweet,
   And with delight we heard the prelude fleet,
And waited for the magic master-word.

In vain we waited—once more silence fell,
   Once more life swept its wonted way along;
   No heroes' deeds are told in deathless song,
No more our hearts are lifted on its swell.

Why are ye silent, O ye who well know
   How thrilling rhyme and lofty thought should
      blend?
   Why fear ye Fame's high places to ascend,
And stand above Fate's idle ebb and flow?

Fear not the loneliness of heart that stings,
   Pause not to rest until the height is gained;
   Fear but to be the coward who remained
Content to grope, although his soul had wings.

Listen, Men in Your Graves

Listen, men under the grasses lying,
   Who fought for the flag on the land and the sea;
Do you hear the bugles wailing and sighing?

Do you hear the fife, insistent and crying?
  Do you hear the drum calling, "follow me?"
O, ye who died where bullets were singing,
  Do you hear the marching feet at your head?
Do you smell the flowers, their incense bringing?
Do you see the banners slowly swinging?
  Do you live today, though we call you dead?

Listen, O men in your graves attended
  By Love and Honor wherever you lie;
Because you have lived life has grown more
      splendid
And we mark where you stood when your brief
      lives ended
  That our country may measure its heroes thereby.

Rest, O ye dead who shall live on for ages,
  Live anew in each breast which valor has known;
Your deeds shall shine out upon earth's whitest
      pages,
Shall be sung by the poets and taught by the
      sages
  Till the world-heart is raised to the height of your
      own.

The Missing Ship

The ships they come and the ships they go
  Far over the shining sea,
But though soft and sweet the south winds blow,

There comes no ship for me.
And though when the harbor bar grows white
　　The sails come swiftly in,
To lie where the waves are calm and bright,
　　Away from the thunderous din,
The bark which carried my hopes and fear
　　Turns not her prow to the shore;
She has sailed the sea for many years,
　　Yet she comes to land no more.

Did she touch at the isles of Might-have-been,
　　Far out to the rosy west?
And before the storm, was she safely in
　　The port of Peace and Rest?
I only know I am growing old
　　With the years that lapse away,
And the hopes I thought always to hold
　　Have left my heart for aye.
But when I reach the Port of Rest,
　　And look o'er the sea once more,
I think that the ship that I loved best
　　Will lie by the shining shore.

The Joy of June

Color and life and scent
All in one glory blent;
Earth, air and heaven in tune—
This is the joy of June.

Night only veils her skies;

When Dawn uplifts her eyes
Out from the drowsy flowers
Rise all the scented hours.

Happy and warm and blest,
This is the whole year's best;
Summer is fair and young,
With sweet songs still unsung.

Shall We Find Them So?

I watched alone the wonder of the night—
The frozen moon, shining with borrowed light,
Trailing upon the lake her silvery bars;
The varying radiance of the distant stars,
Set jewel-like in the great azure arch,
Yet ever moving, with majestic march,
To great Arcturus, throned upon the sky,
Watching processions of the worlds wheel by,
And wondered if with equal, far-seen grace,
Our planet in these mighty ranks keeps place.
I heard the voices of the brooding night—
The hum of creatures whom the days affright;
The querulous katydid's incessant note,
The flute-like call from the shy Hylas' throat;
From the far ponds a faint, unchanging drone,
To other sounds a cadenced undertone;
My heart grew faint, and I felt tears arise,
So great the beauty of the earth and skies;
If there are fairer worlds than this to know,
If we forget not, shall we find them so?

The Beautiful Old Earth

They may tell us of earth's ages—she is very old,
    in truth—
But she bears the charm forever of a fair, perpet-
    ual youth.
Year by year I hold her dearer, with a deep,
    admiring love,
And with fresh delight each morning see her fair
    processions move.
Tender spring time, fervid summer, royal autumn,
    winter stern,
Each has many a hidden beauty, which a lifetime
    cannot learn.
O the secrets of the forest, which it whispers in
    the ear
When its stately aisles are trodden, with no other
    mortal near!
O the beauty of the sunset, when the day-god goes
    to rest
On a bed of glory, curtained with the splendor of
    the west!
O the silence and the marvel of the strange, en-
    chanting night,
With the silver lamps of heaven burning with their
    solemn light!
O the wild, lamenting waters, moving on from
    shore to shore,
Seeking rest and peace forever—finding it, ah,
    nevermore!

Who can learn the tale they tell us through their
     billows, o'er and o'er,
Or give voice unto the meaning of Niagara's
     ceaseless roar?
And the ever haunting wonder of the winds that
     sweep and swell—
Will they always be forbidden all their mysteries
     to tell?
And the rainbow, curving softly o'er the mountains
     and the glen,
Like a shining bridge to heaven for the feet of
     weary men!
Who that sees the changing streamers of the
     Borealis' flame
But must bow in awe and wonder to a force he
     cannot name?
Or what mortal, though he study for a lifetime,
     ever knows
Even the secret of the color that is hidden in the
     rose?
Though she cares not for our homage, knows not
     of our praise or love,
But goes on her way unheeding with the shining
     orbs above,
I shall love the earth forever, till they lay me down
     to rest
Hidden by the emerald mantle, folded closely to
     her breast!

Dreams

O dreams, sad dreams that come with sleep and
    night,
  Of lights which shone upon youth's flower-decked
    shore,
  Of dear, dead days, of faces seen no more,
And tones which waken all the old delight '
We knew when hours were fleet and days were
    bright;
  Sweet as sweet Love, with all his lying lore;
  Sad as the lonely life which waits before,
Memory's handmaiden, with her sword of might—

Which are ye, curse or blessing? Who can tell
  Who longs for night through all the lonely day—
Who hears in dreams alone sweet voices swell
  Which made the music of life's earlier day?
And, ah! What matter? for we near a home
Where waits a bed to which dreams never come.

Easter Lilies

I saw the gracefull lily-bells a-swinging in the light,
I heard the snowy lily-bells a-singing in the night;
"Break out in bloom, O lagging buds," 'twas this I
    heard them say—
"Tomorrow's dawn will bring to us the blessed
    Easter day.
"Because we are most beautiful, with chalices that
    bear

A message from the heavenly world to this of grief
    and care,
Men choose us for their messenger, to breath their
    prayers to him
Who rose from death to give them hope, and light
    where all was dim."

O happy, happy lilies, who bear, your cups within,
The hopes and prayers of hearts that break with
    sorrow and with sin,
Before His feet who stands among the asphodels
    of heaven,
I pray you lay my burning tears, which plead for
    sins forgiven.

Midsummer

Now has the year come into its glory,
    'Tis the high tide of its beauty and bliss;
Every day tells a wonderful story
    And promises hours sweeter than this.

The hum of bees and children's laughter,
    The song of birds and rippling streams,—
How we shall miss and long for them after,—
    How they will echoe through all our dreams.

Think not now of the white snows falling,
    Of days grown short and nights grown chill;
Summer is Queen and her voice is calling—
    Listen, and love her, and do her will.

In the Garden

` "And they heard the voice of the Lord God walking in the garden in the cool of the day." (Genesis 3:8.)

The Lord walked in the garden;
Though spreading •far, from east to west
　　The universe upheld his throne,
Creation offered of its best,
　　And heaven was all his own.
The Lord walked in the garden.

The Lord walked in the garden;
The brooding silence of the night
　　Descended on the dewy flowers,
And he whose word created light
　　Found pleasure in the bowers—
The Lord walked in the garden.

The Lord walked in the garden;
O, holy comfort of the stars
　　And wonderous mystery of night;
For, passing through the ether's bars
　　And leaving heaven's own light,
The Lord walked in the garden.

INDEX

CPSIA information can be obtained
at www.ICGtesting.com
Printed in the USA
BVHW08*1523041018
529297BV00008B/250/P